LIFE'S BITTER POOL

Books by Derek Prince

Appointment in Jerusalem
Atonement: Your Appointment with God
Blessing or Curse: You Can Choose
Called to Conquer
Choice of a Partner, The
Complete Salvation
Declaring God's Word
Derek Prince—A Biography by Stephen Mansfield
Derek Prince: On Experiencing God's Power
Destiny Of Israel and The Church,
Divine Exchange, The
Does Your Tongue Need Healing?
End of Life's Journey, The
Entering the Presence of God
Expelling Demons
Explaining Blessings and Curses
Extravagant Love
Faith to Live By
Fasting
First Mile, The
Foundations For Christian Living
Gateway to God's Blessing
Gifts of the Spirit, The
God Is a Matchmaker
God's Medicine Bottle
God's Plan for Your Money
God's Remedy for Rejection
God's Will for Your Life
God's Word Heals
Grace of Yielding, The
Harvest Just Ahead, The
Holy Spirit in You, The
How to Fast Successfully
Husbands and Fathers
I Forgive You
Judging
Laying the Foundations Series
Life's Bitter Pool
Lucifer Exposed
Marriage Covenant, The
Orphans, Widows, the Poor and Oppressed
Our Debt to Israel
Pages from My Life's Book
Partners for Life
Philosophy, the Bible and the Supernatural
Power in the Name
Power of the Sacrifice, The
Prayers and Proclamations
Praying for the Government
Protection from Deception
Promise of Provision, The
Promised Land
Prophetic Guide to the End Times
Receiving God's Best
Rediscovering God's Church
Rules of Engagement
Secrets of a Prayer Warrior
Self-Study Bible Course (revised and expanded)
Set Apart For God
Shaping History Through Prayer and Fasting
Spiritual Warfare
Surviving the Last Days
They Shall Expel Demons
Through the Psalms with Derek Prince
War in Heaven
Who Is the Holy Spirit?
You Matter to God
You Shall Receive Power

Derek Prince

Life's Bitter Pool

Derek Prince Ministries–International
www.derekprince.com

LIFE'S BITTER POOL

© 1984 Derek Prince Ministries – International

This edition DPM-UK 2012
All rights reserved.

Published by DPM-UK
Kingsfield, Hadrian Way,
Baldock, SG7 6AN, UK

www.dpmuk.org

ISBN 978-1-908594-52-5
Product Code: T84

Unless otherwise specified, all Scriptures are taken from the *New International Version* of the Bible © 1978 by New York International Bible Society. All Scriptures marked NASB are taken from the *New American Standard Bible*, © The Lockman Foundation 1960, 1962, 1963, 1971, 1973.

This book is an edited transcript of *Life's Bitter Pool* from the *Today With Derek Prince* daily radio programme.

No part of this book may be reproduced or transmitted in any form or by any means, electronic or mechanical, including photocopying, recording, or by means of any information storage and retrieval system, without permission in writing from the publisher.

Derek Prince Ministries
www.derekprince.com

CONTENTS

	Introduction	7
1	The Purpose of Testing	13
2	The Healing Tree	19
3	The Lord Our Healer	25
4	Death Before Resurrection	31
	About the Author	37
	Derek Prince Ministries Offices Worldwide	40

INTRODUCTION

This teaching is based on an incident in the history of God's people, Israel, just after they had been miraculously delivered out of Egypt and had passed through the waters of the Red Sea as though on dry land. The incident is recorded in Exodus 15:19-26. First, we will look at the climax of their miraculous deliverance in Exodus 15:19-21:

> *When Pharaoh's horses, chariots and horsemen went into the sea, the Lord brought the waters of the sea back over them, but the Israelites walked through the sea on dry ground. Then Miriam the prophetess, Aaron's sister, took a tambourine in her hand, and all the women followed her, with tambourines and dancing. Miriam sang to them:*
>
> *"Sing to the Lord, for he is highly exalted. The horse and its rider he has hurled into the sea."* NIV

That really was a tremendous triumph, wasn't it? Israel had passed through the waters of the Red Sea miraculously as if on dry ground. Then their enemy, the Egyptians, had followed them in, and God had brought the waters back over the Egyptians, swept them away, and put an end to that entire force of the enemy that was pursuing His people. Not one Egyptian survived.

I am sure the Israelites concluded that now all their troubles were over and the rest of their journey to the Promised Land would be easy and uneventful. As a result, they were unprepared for what lay ahead. This is what followed after this tremendous deliverance – in Exodus 15:22-24:

> *Then Moses led Israel from the Red Sea and they went into the Desert of Shur. For three days they travelled in the desert without finding water. When they came to Marah, they could not drink its water because it was bitter. (That is why the place is called Marah.)* [In Hebrew, Marah is the word for bitter.] *So the people grumbled against Moses, saying, "What are we to drink?"* NIV

Picture that scene for a moment: they had experienced a glorious deliverance; they were triumphant, exulting; they felt everything was under God's control. Then it says they were led into the wilderness of Shur, led by God through Moses. In that wilderness they went three days without finding water. Of course, they had an emergency supply of water with them in water skins, but they must have been running low. The children and the cattle were beginning to become thirsty; they were all weary with the hot and dusty journey.

Then in the distance they saw the gleam of water in this pool called Marah. Some of them must have started to run to get there to quench their thirst. But, oh, what a bitter disappointment when they stooped down to drink! The waters were so bitter they could not drink.

The people were totally unprepared for that situation. They could not conceive that such a thing would happen to them when God was actually leading them and when God had just granted them such a tremendous deliverance and victory.

The people were unprepared, but there was one person who was not unprepared, and that was God. Let me tell you, no matter how many times we may feel unprepared, God is never unprepared. God never has an emergency. God is never confronted with a situation for which He has no answer.

Now the people grumbled but one man, Moses, had the sense to pray. Scholars estimate that there were probably around three million Israelites there. Think of the noise of three million people all grumbling at one time! I'm sure it must have been hard for Moses to hear his own voice in prayer. But Moses did the sensible thing – he prayed – and this is what followed (Exodus 15:25-26):

> *Then Moses cried out to the Lord, and the Lord showed him a piece of wood* [a tree]. *He threw it into the water, and the water became sweet. There the Lord made a decree and a law for them, and there he tested them. He said, "If you listen carefully to the voice of the Lord your God and do what is right in his eyes, if you pay attention to his commands and keep all his decrees, I will not bring on you any of the diseases I brought on the Egyptians, for I am the Lord who heals you."* NIV

First of all, I need to say a word about the word "tree." In the Hebrew language, the word for "tree" is used for a tree while it is growing, but it is still used for a tree when it has been cut down – when it becomes a long plank or a beam. It is not indicated from the words here whether the tree was growing and Moses had to cut it down or whether it was a tree that had fallen. But whatever it was, it was the key to the situation. When Moses picked up that tree and threw it into the water, the water became sweet.

It is important to see that the Scripture does not say the tree made the water sweet. There was nothing magical about the tree. It was the supernatural power of God that made the water sweet. The casting in of the tree was the act of faith that released the miracle-working power of God into the water. That is how God's miracle-working power is usually released in our lives. It takes a specific act of faith to release the miracle-working power. The act of faith is the key that unlocks the miracle-working power of God and makes it available in the situation where we need it.

This particular principle is illustrated many times in the ministry of the prophet Elisha, further on in the Old Testament. For instance, there was a stream near Jericho of which the waters were bad; it made the ground infertile, the people could not drink it. Elisha just took some salt, threw it into the water, and said, "This is what the Lord says: 'I have healed this water,' " and it was healed. (See 2 Kings 2:19-21.) The water was healed not by the salt, but by the supernatural power of God. Casting the salt into the water released the supernatural power of God. That is the principle. The act of faith is the key that unlocks the miracle-working power of God. Interestingly enough, you can go to Jericho today and still see that stream flowing. They call it Elisha's Stream. The water is still pure and fresh today. So that was a miracle that had a long-lasting effect.

In another situation, Elisha was confronted by some food that had been poisoned. The people were about to suffer, perhaps even die. Elisha took some flour, threw it into the pot and said, in effect, "The pot is healed." (See 2 Kings 4:38-41.) It wasn't the flour that counteracted the poison, it was the supernatural power of God. The supernatural power of God was released by that act of faith.

And so it was, here, with these bitter waters. Moses threw the tree in and that act of throwing in the tree released the power of God that turned the bitter waters into sweet.

This story, of course, goes back three thousand years, but the truths it contains are as vivid and as real today as in the time of Moses. We will begin to look together at some of these truths to see how they apply to our own lives and our own situations.

Two lessons stand out for me from this story of the bitter pool that we just looked at. The first lesson is: great victories prepare us for great testings. The fact that God has given you a tremendous deliverance – a tremendous victory, blessing, healing, or whatever it may be – does not mean that the rest of your life is going to be without further testing. Rather, the greater the victory, the greater will be the test that you are able to face on the basis of that victory. That was Israel's mistake. They thought that, just because they had had this tremendous deliverance, nothing else could happen that would ever challenge their faith. Consequently, they were not ready when they came to the bitter pool. Instead of praying, they grumbled.

The second lesson – and this is vital – is that the bitter pool was in God's programme. God actually led them to the bitter pool. He had a purpose in bringing them to that bitter pool, and this is true in our lives. God, from time to time, permits us to be confronted with a bitter pool, but He has a purpose.

Let me just give you a few contemporary examples of the kind of bitter pool that you and I may have to face. The first example I think of is a broken marriage. Alas, how many people today have had to face the bitter pool of a marriage that has ended in divorce: the bitterness, the agony, the embarrassment. The wounds that are left are so deep in the human personality.

Another kind of bitter pool is a business failure. Perhaps you may have worked for years to build up some kind of business and establish yourself financially. Then, through circumstances you could not control (the economy changed, etc.), you found yourself penniless, maybe quite well on in life. That is a bitter pool.

You may have had a health breakdown; a physical breakdown or, worse still, a mental or emotional breakdown. Now you are trying to put together the broken pieces of a life that was strong and healthy and victorious.

Another kind of bitter pool is disillusionment with a human leader. You may have followed somebody, given them your best in service. It may be a religious leader, a political leader, or it might even be a parent. This person in whom you had confidence, whom you looked up to, suddenly, one day, was not what he seemed to be: he had feet of clay, he failed you. Your confidence was misplaced.

I would like to ask you a question: Are you willing to learn the lessons God has for you in the bitter pool? If so, you need to read the rest of the sections in this book.

I have painted for you a picture of Israel's disappointment. They had had a glorious victory. No doubt they felt that all their problems had been settled once and for all. Then they went three days in the desert without finding water; they were thirsty, hot, weary, discouraged. They saw this pool of water gleaming there in the sun, but when they ran to it and stooped to drink, it was too bitter for them to drink! It was a terrible, bitter disappointment.

The people were unprepared, you see. They assumed that everything was going to be easy from then on, there would be no more tests of their faith. But God was not unprepared; God knew what to do; He had the answer. The people grumbled and got nothing; Moses prayed and God showed Him the answer. God had that tree ready; He knew what had to be done, but it was only through prayer that Moses could find the solution.

In speaking to large and small congregations at different times, I have often asked people, "How many of you have had to struggle with disappointment?" Very few people in such a congregation would ever say, "I've never confronted disappointment." It is one of the things that comes our way, and I would like for you to understand and learn how to face disappointments and get the best out of them.

I previously pointed out two lessons that apply from that story for you and me today. The first lesson is that great victories prepare us for great testings; they do not indicate that there will be no more testing. The second lesson is that the bitter pool was in God's programme; He led them there, He had a purpose.

Then I pointed out that we still come to bitter pools in our lives today and I gave you some examples: a broken marriage, a business failure, a health breakdown, disillusionment with a human leader, or perhaps even with a parent.

1
THE PURPOSE OF TESTING

Now I will make a further application with this story and address the purpose of testing. You see, the question in our lives is not whether we will experience testing, but only *how we will respond* to the testing. The testing there at Marah exposed an area in the character of the Israelites that needed to be dealt with; an area that was expressed in grumbling.

Let me tell you this: the Bible has nothing good anywhere to say about grumbling. Grumbling is a way, not to solve your problems, but to magnify them. You will never find the way out of your problems by grumbling. If, when you come under pressure, you begin to grumble, then you are like the Israelites. There is an area in your character that needs to be dealt with. God knew that area was there all along, but He had to let you come to the bitter pool so that you could find out what was really inside you. Actually, the act of grumbling indicates a lack of faith, a lack of gratitude, self-centredness – many serious problems that hinder our further progress in the Lord.

The Lord had a lot farther for Israel to go than the pool of Marah. He really was taking them to the land that He had promised, but they weren't fit to make the full journey to the Promised Land until that thing in their character, which was exposed at Marah, had been dealt with. So, when you come to your Marah, your bitter waters, and you begin to grumble, realise that there is something in you that must be dealt with and that God brought you to that place so He might deal with that thing, but He can only deal with it if you co-operate.

The Bible warns us clearly that we are going to experience testing; it is stated many times. One particularly clear passage is in the epistle of James 1:2-4:

> *Consider it pure joy, my brothers, whenever you face trials of many kinds. . . .* NIV

I never read those words without asking myself, "Is that how I react to trials of many kinds?" Is that how you react to trials of many kinds? When you are walking with the Lord and you are confronted with all sorts of trials, do you consider it pure joy? Do you say, "Hallelujah! Praise God for this trial!"? Or do you do what the Israelites did – begin to grumble, "Lord, why did you let that happen? God, I thought you had this situation in control. Now I don't know what to do."

James continues:

> *. . . because you know that the testing of your faith develops perseverance. Perseverance must finish its work so that you may be mature and complete, not lacking anything.* NIV

One essential element in Christian character is perseverance. Until we achieve perseverance, there are goals in God that we can never attain. Perseverance is brought out by testing our faith. There is really only one way to learn perseverance and that is by persevering. In order to persevere you have to be in a situation where perseverance is needed.

James says, "Perseverance must finish its work so that you may be mature and complete, not lacking anything." That is God's goal for you: to be mature, fully grown up, complete, having a fully-rounded Christian character, not lacking anything. Do you want that? Do you want to be mature and complete, not lacking anything? How could you wish anything else? If you do want this, you have to go through the process; and the process may include your particular Marah or bitter pool.

When encountering a bitter pool, there are just two alternative responses: the people grumbled, that was the response of unbelief; Moses prayed, that was the response of faith. Which will you do? The next time you come to that bitter pool, which are you going to do?

On the shore of the bitter pool Moses prayed and cried out to the Lord. There was no other source of help but the Lord. And when Moses took that course to pray, rather than to grumble – the response of faith, rather than the response of unbelief – God responded with a new revelation of Himself.

That was God's purpose in bringing Israel to the bitter pool. He had something for them to learn and He set them in a situation where the revelation He had for them would be appropriate. He responded with a revelation of Himself.

It was a double revelation which I will deal with more fully later. First of all, He revealed to them the tree – the means of healing. Second, and more important still, He revealed Himself to them in a new aspect: the Lord their Healer. That was His ultimate objective in that experience at the bitter pool.

I want to point out a principle which has been summed up very succinctly in a statement that I heard somebody make once. Actually, I really didn't like the statement when I heard it the first time because I thought, This doesn't suggest that life is going to be the way I'd like it to be! The statement is this: "Man's disappointments are God's appointments."

As I stated previously, a disappointment is one of the things that nearly all of us face. Disappointment really is a bitter pool. When your hopes are set high – you are moving forward and everything seems to be going right – and then it all falls apart and crumbles, you are left with nothing but disappointed hopes. That is a bitter pool.

What I want you to grasp is this: God led you to that bitter pool. He has something good for you at the bitter pool if you respond the right way. "Man's disappointments are God's appointments."

It has something to do with human nature. When everything is going well and life is pretty easy, most of us tend to be somewhat superficial. We will be content with the status quo; content to go to church and pay our tithes and say our prayers and lead a fairly respectable kind of life. But God has something much further and much deeper for us. Somehow or another, He gets us to the bitter pool. Then, in the depths of agony and disappointment, we cry out as Moses did. When we do, we get a much deeper and fuller revelation of God, which only comes on the shores of the bitter pool.

If you have faced a bitter pool in the past or if you are now facing a bitter pool, just bear in mind that "Your disappointment is God's appointment."

I have pointed out a number of lessons from that Old Testament story, which is three thousand years old and more, but the lessons are still up-to-date and relevant for you and me today.

First of all, great victories prepare us for great testings. The fact that we have had a great victory does not mean we will never be tested again; rather, it means we will be better equipped for the next test.

Second, the bitter pool was in God's programme. He had a purpose in bringing His people there. It was He who led them there, and this is often true in our lives. The bitter pool is part of God's programme. He has a purpose.

Third, the question is not whether we will experience testing, but only how we will respond to the testing.

Fourth, in this case at the bitter pool, there were two alternative responses: the people grumbled, Moses prayed. The people who grumbled got nothing; the man who prayed got the answer.

The next principle is: to Moses' prayer of faith, God in turn responded with a new revelation of Himself. That was God's purpose: to bring His people to the place where they could receive the revelation that He had for them. I have summed that up in the little phrase, "Man's disappointments are God's appointments."

2
THE HEALING TREE

Now we will look at the revelation that God had for His people there at the bitter pool. There were two aspects to the revelation: the first was the revelation of the healing tree; the second was the revelation of God the Healer.

We will start by looking back at the particular verse in Exodus 15 which speaks about that tree: Exodus 15:25:

> *Then he* [Moses] *cried out to the Lord, and the Lord showed him a tree; and he threw it into the waters, and the waters became sweet.* NASB

So the solution to the problem was found in that tree.

Now that tree speaks of one of the main themes in the entire Bible. It speaks of another tree that was raised, perhaps 2,400 years later, on a hill called Golgotha: the cross. Whenever you read in the Bible about a tree, you should be alert to see if it is really a reference to the cross of Jesus.

We need to understand the Hebrew use of the word "tree" which I touched on previously. In the Hebrew language the word for "tree" is used for a tree when it is growing, but it is still used for a tree after it has been cut down. When it is just a long pole or some such thing, it is still referred to as a tree. So a tree can also be a gibbet, a gallows or a cross.

There are several examples of this; we will look at a few of them. First of all, in the book of Deuteronomy 21:22-23:

> *If a man guilty of a capital offence is put to death and his body is hung on a tree, you must not leave his body on the tree overnight. Be sure to bury him that same day, because anyone who is hung on a tree is under God's curse.* NIV

So there was a way of executing a person which was often followed in the Old Testament: the person was hung on a tree. Sometimes he was killed first and then hung on the tree and sometimes he was killed by hanging him on the tree. But the Law of Moses stated that no man must ever be left hanging on a tree overnight because anyone who hangs on a tree is a curse.

You will remember in the record of the crucifixion of Jesus, after Jesus had died on the cross, the Jewish religious leaders went to Pontius Pilate and asked him if the body might be taken down because they did not want it to remain there over the following holy day. They did not want that curse displayed on a holy day.

Paul takes this ordinance of the Old Testament in the book of Deuteronomy and, in the epistle to the Galatians, he uses it to interpret the full significance of the death of Jesus on the cross. This is what Paul says in Galatians 3:13-14:

> *Christ redeemed us from the curse of the law by becoming a curse for us, for it is written: "Cursed is everyone who is hung on a tree."* [That is a quotation from the passage in Deuteronomy I just quoted.] *He* [Christ] *redeemed us in order that the blessing given to Abraham might come to the Gentiles through Christ Jesus, so that by faith we might receive the promise of the Spirit.* NIV

You see, in God's purpose of redemption, Jesus was permitted to become a curse. He took the curse that was due to a lost, fallen race – to our Adamic race. He became the curse that He might redeem us from the curse and in place of the curse, we might inherit the blessing. The evidence that Jesus became a curse for us was that He was hung on the tree, on the cross. Those who knew the Word of God from the Old Testament knew that in that act Jesus, in the purpose of God, became a curse that we might receive the blessing.

There is the exchange: Jesus became the curse that we might receive the blessing. It is like the waters of Marah: Jesus took the bitter that we might be able to drink the sweet; He took the curse that we might have the blessing.

When you think of the tree that was cast into the water, think of the cross of Jesus and the fact that on that cross Jesus took the bitter curse that we might have the sweetness of the blessing. Moses casting the tree into the pool is an example, pattern or picture of you and me taking what was accomplished on our behalf on the cross and using it to make our bitter pool sweet.

I would also like to quote a passage in 1 Peter 2:24, where again the cross is referred to as a tree and the same truth is brought out.

> *He himself* [Jesus] *bore our sins in his body on the tree, so that we might die to sins and live for righteousness; by his wounds you have been healed.* NIV

Again, Jesus became sin that we might receive His righteousness; He was wounded that we might be healed. All of this is brought out in the use of the word "tree" for the cross. It was on that "tree" that full healing was obtained for the whole human race: spiritual healing from sin, physical healing from sickness, deliverance from the curse, the right to inherit the blessing. All of this was accomplished through that tree, which is the cross.

As you picture in your mind Moses casting the tree into the bitter water that it might be made sweet, then you should picture yourself taking the truth of the cross, applying it in your life and turning your bitter pool into sweetness.

The healing and the deliverance that come from the tree, which is the cross – the cross of Jesus – must be applied in our lives by an act of faith. Just as Moses, by an act of faith, threw that tree into the bitter water, so we, too, must exercise faith when we confront that bitter pool. We must have faith in what Jesus accomplished on the cross and, metaphorically, take that tree and throw it into our bitter pool. It must be an act of faith to release the miracle-working power that is in the cross of Jesus Christ: power to make the bitter waters sweet.

I want to suggest to you certain very simple, practical steps that you can take in your life if you are confronted by the bitter pool to change that bitter pool into sweet. First of all, recognise that the bitter pool is in God's programme. God led you there, He knows all about it, and He has the remedy.

Second, let God deal with any defects in your character that have been exposed by the bitter pool. If you have grumbled when you should have prayed, bear in mind there is something in you that must be dealt with by the Holy Spirit.

Third, by faith accept what Jesus did for you on the cross. "He himself bore our sins in his body on the tree, so that we might die to sins and live for righteousness; by his wounds you have been healed." It is not: "You will be healed"; but: "You have been healed." As far as God is concerned, it is already done; it is finished, it is accomplished.

Here is the fourth and vital step: begin to thank God for what Jesus has done on your behalf. Begin to receive by thanking Him for whatever it is you need: forgiveness, healing (whether it is emotional or physical), release from resentment, bitterness, rebellion, confusion. Thanking God, in faith, corresponds to throwing that tree into the water. The purest expression of faith that you and I are capable of is simply thanking God – not seeing any change, not waiting for the evidence, but believing what God says about the cross of Jesus – and then beginning to thank Him for what was done on our behalf on the cross. Thanking Him releases that miracle-working power to change the bitter water to sweet.

Here are some of the main lessons that we have noted so far.

First, great victories prepare us for great testing.

Second, the bitter pool was in God's programme; He had a purpose; it was He who brought them to the very shore of the bitter pool.

Third, the question is not whether we will experience testing, but only how we will respond to testing.

Fourth, two alternative responses are indicated in this incident: the people grumbled and Moses prayed; the people got nothing, Moses got the answer.

Fifth, to Moses' prayer of faith, God, in turn, responded with a new revelation of Himself. That was God's purpose: He wanted to bring His people there so that He might give them this further, deeper, fuller revelation of Himself.

In the previous section, we looked at the first aspect of the revelation: the healing tree. I pointed out that the word "tree" in Hebrew is used of a tree whether it is growing or whether it is cut down; it is used of a gallows, a gibbet; it is also used of the cross. The tree that made the bitter waters sweet is, for you and me, a picture of the cross of Jesus. On the cross, Jesus was made a curse. The Old Testament says: ". . . cursed is everyone that hangeth on a tree." Jesus received the curse that we might receive the blessing. Jesus drank the bitter that we might enjoy the sweet. On the cross He was wounded that we might be healed. On the cross every human need was met by the substitutionary, atoning, sacrificial death of Jesus Christ. That is the healing tree – the revelation of what was accomplished for you and me by the death of Jesus on the tree which was the cross.

3
THE LORD OUR HEALER

I want to look at the second aspect of the revelation: the Lord our Healer. In every spiritual experience in which we relate to God, when we receive provision from God, we always need to look beyond the provision to the Provider. The provision was the tree, but the Provider was the Lord. The Lord did not allow Israel merely to receive the revelation of the tree, but the revelation of the tree led up to the revelation of the Lord as their Healer. I will quote again the words of Exodus 15:25-26:

> *Then he* [Moses] *cried out to the Lord, and the Lord showed him a tree; and he threw it into the waters, and the waters became sweet. There He made for them a statute and regulation, and there He tested them. And He said, "If you will give earnest heed to the voice of the Lord your God, and do what is right in His sight, and give ear to His commandments, and keep all His statutes, I will put none of the diseases on you which I have put on the Egyptians; for I, the Lord, am your healer* [or 'I am the Lord your healer']*.*" NASB

The ultimate revelation was not a revelation of a provision, but a revelation of the Provider. That is a very important principle of which you need to lay hold: every revelation of God, if we follow it through to its intended conclusion, will bring us to God Himself. "I am the Lord your healer."

The word that is translated "healer" is the modern Hebrew word for a doctor. It has not changed in over three thousand years and that is exactly what it means. We need to understand that. The Lord desires to be His people's doctor, their physician. It was that revelation for which He was preparing His people when He brought them to the pool. A revelation is not something that the natural mind can receive. Normally, we have to come into some kind of a situation where we need the revelation.

Many years ago, I myself lay for one year on end in a hospital with a condition that the doctors were not able to heal. In that situation, through the Bible and through the Holy Spirit, the Lord revealed Himself to me as my doctor. "I am the Lord your healer [your doctor, physician]." That is the revelation to which He is bringing us.

One thing we must understand is that God never changes. He not merely was His people's doctor, He is His people's doctor. Malachi 3:6, right at the end of the old covenant, says:

> *"I the Lord do not change* [or 'I am the Lord, I do not change']." NIV

He was, He is, He will be: He doesn't change – our Healer, our Physician.

Then in the New Testament, Hebrews 13:8:

> *Jesus Christ is the same yesterday and today and forever.* NIV

So many times we can believe for yesterday and we can believe for forever, but what about today? We can believe it happened in the Bible and it will happen when we get to heaven, but let us not forget: it is for today, too. Today, Jesus Christ is the same as He was when He was on earth. Today, God is the same as He was at the bitter pool. He is our physician, our doctor, our healer.

There is one verse in the New Testament that especially describes the ministry of Jesus on earth which, I think, says it more completely in one verse than anywhere else I know. It is Acts 10:38. Peter is speaking to the household of Cornelius and he is describing the ministry of Jesus on earth as he himself witnessed it.

> *. . . God anointed Jesus of Nazareth with the Holy Spirit and power, and how he went around doing good and healing all who were under the power of the devil, because God was with him.* NIV

What blesses me is we have all three persons of the eternal Godhead: God the Father anointed Jesus the Son with the Holy Spirit. What was the result? It was healing, liberation, deliverance, wholeness for everybody that Jesus came in contact with. It seems to me, if I can say it reverently, that there is almost a jealousy between the persons of the Godhead when it comes to blessing the human race. Not one of them wants to be left out. The Father anointed the Son with the Spirit, that all of them might share in this ministry of mercy and deliverance and making people whole. This is the revelation of God's eternal nature. God had allowed His people to come to a place of need at the waters of Marah, so that they might receive the revelation.

Today, if you are in a place of need, if you feel that you are faced with those bitter waters, I want to suggest to you that you take this attitude: God permitted this. God is in this. He has a programme. I won't grumble, I'll pray. I'll wait on God and allow Him to speak to me. I'll let Him show me the revelation that He has for me in this situation.

I want to emphasise once more that the full purpose of God was not merely to reveal the tree, but to reveal Himself. I think this needs to be said to multitudes of Christians today. We are never intended by God to stop short at an experience, a doctrine, a revelation, or a blessing. Thank God for every one of those things that we receive, but we cannot rest in them. Each one of them, in a sense, is somewhat impersonal and impermanent. What we need, in the last resort, is a person. And every true doctrine or revelation we receive will always lead us in the end to the person of God Himself.

I want you to follow me in just a few Scriptures from the Old and New Testaments that bring out this principle. In Exodus 19:4 God said to Israel:

> *"You yourselves have seen what I did to Egypt, and how I carried you on eagles' wings and brought you to myself."* NIV

Notice, the purpose of God was to bring Israel to Himself – not just to the Law, not just to a covenant, not just to the Promised Land – but to Himself. That is always God's purpose.

And then in Psalm 73:26, the psalmist says:

> *My flesh and my heart may fail,*
> *but God is the strength of my heart*
> *and my portion forever.* NIV

God is my portion; not some blessing, not some experience, not some revelation. God is my portion. I will not settle for anything less than God Himself.

Isaiah 12:2:

> *"Surely God is my salvation; I will trust and not be afraid. The Lord, the Lord, is my strength and my song; he has become my salvation.* NIV

That is a revelation. When you can say the Lord is my salvation – not the church, not a doctrine, not an experience, but the Lord – there you will be secure; there you will have come to the fullness of the revelation. Don't stop short at the tree. Don't stop short at the experience. No matter how blessed they may be, always move on to the revelation of the Lord Himself.

And then those beautiful words of Jesus in Matthew 11:28:

"Come to me, all you who are weary and burdened, and I will give you rest." NIV

This is the ultimate invitation. "Come to me . . . I will give you rest." Don't stop short at anything less than God manifested in Jesus Himself. Come to Him. He will give you rest.

You see, the human heart craves a person. The human heart can never be satisfied with something impersonal. Ultimately, we need a person, and God is the person that every one of us needs and must also come to know.

Life's bitter pool has been based on the experience of the Israelites in the desert when they came to the pool of Marah and found the water too bitter to drink. I have suggested to you that there is a bitter pool somewhere in the life of nearly every one of us; a place of bitter disappointment where something that gleams and shines and seems so beautiful is not really what we thought it would be.

Some examples of bitter pools that are common in our contemporary culture today are: a broken marriage, a business failure, a health breakdown, or disillusionment with a human leader. We saw, as we studied the incident in the history of Israel, that the bitter pool was in God's programme for Israel. I believe the same can be true in the life of each one of us. God permits us to come to the bitter pool because He has a purpose. Then, when God's purpose is accomplished, the bitter, through the supernatural Word of God, turns to sweet if we respond aright to God's dealings. It is of utmost importance that we respond aright.

4
DEATH BEFORE RESURRECTION

In this section, I will express this vital truth of our experience as a comprehensive principle that operates in every area of life. In fact, I would say that God has built this principle into the operation of the universe itself. There are two passages that I particularly have in mind that state the principles. The first is found in the Old Testament; the second, which we will look at later, is found in the New.

The first passage is found in Hosea 2:14-16. This is a prophetic passage which I believe is coming into fulfilment in our day. It is the promise of God to His people, Israel, to restore them – to restore them to Himself, restore them to the blessings that He has for them, and restore them to their land. Here in Hosea He describes the way that He is going to work out their restoration. Read this carefully because, as so often happens, the way God does things is not the way you and I would expect Him to do things. Therefore we must be watchful or we will miss what God is doing. The Lord says:

"Therefore I am now going to allure her; I will lead her into the desert and speak tenderly to her."

The word "allure" is a rather mystical word. It contains the thought of somehow dealing with us in a way that we do not fully understand and yet we feel drawn.

He says, "I will lead her into the desert . . . " (the desert is not normally the place of blessing) ". . . and speak tenderly to her." Literally in Hebrew the Lord says, "I will speak to her heart." This is a very beautiful expression in Hebrew. But, you see, it is not always possible for God to speak to our heart. Sometimes our heart is closed. Sometimes we are not responsive. So God has to work in our lives and bring about situations (like bringing Israel into the desert) where He can speak to our heart.

Then this is what God says once He has gained Israel's attention:

> *"There I will give her back her vineyards, and will make the Valley of Achor a door of hope. There she will sing as in the days of her youth, as in the day she came up out of Egypt."*

In the Hebrew, the word Achor means "trouble." "I will make the Valley of *Trouble* a door of hope." The phrase "door of hope" in Hebrew is *Petah Tikva*. It is the name of one of the major suburbs of Tel Aviv today and is taken from this passage in Hosea.

We saw earlier in the story of the bitter pool how Miriam and all the women of Israel sang praises right there on the shores of the Red Sea. God says, here in Hosea, "I'm going to give her back a song." Maybe some of you have lost the song. It is tragic when a Christian loses that song. You used to have a song in your heart; you used to praise the Lord so freely and spontaneously. But now there is a heaviness, there is doubt, or a sense of being left out. God wants to give you back your song.

> *"There she will sing as in the days of her youth, as in the day she came up out of Egypt.*

At this point, we come to the purpose of God, to His revelation. Just as at the bitter pool, there is a revelation of Himself that God wants to give.

> *"In that day," declares the Lord, "you will call me 'my husband'; you will no longer call me 'my master.'"* NIV

Under the Old Covenant, Israel's relationship to the Lord was a marriage relationship, but they knew Him as Baal, as Master. It was a relationship not really based on heart commitment, on deep personal love. But God says when He restores you, you will not come back on the same level of revelation, but on a higher revelation. You won't just call Him, "my Master," but you will call Him, "my husband." "Husband" is a very intimate word in Hebrew. What God is saying, in effect, is: "I'll show you myself in a new light. I'll show you myself as the one who loves you as a husband loves his wife." It is a revelation of love and of deep tenderness.

God's purpose in dealing with Israel was to bring them to a new revelation of Himself. When I see in history all the infinite wisdom and patience of God which He has expended in dealing with Israel (and is still expending), I take tremendous courage in my own life. If God is so patient with the nation of Israel, then He can be that patient with me. Even if I must go through the Valley of Trouble, if I will continue and persevere – not give up, not turn back, not grumble, not start to complain – then that Valley of Trouble will become for me, as for Israel, a Door of Hope. A door that leads me to a new and deeper and fuller revelation of the Lord; a revelation of His love and His compassion and His tenderness. Sometimes it is only in seasons of grief that we can really appreciate compassion and tenderness.

If you have a bitter pool, bear in mind that out of the bitter pool God is going to reveal Himself to you if you will let Him speak to your heart.

Now I want to illustrate the same principle of God's dealing from a passage in the New Testament. Paul is writing in a very personal vein about experiences that he himself had gone through; very hard, difficult experiences. The passage is found in 2 Corinthians 1:8-10:

> *We do not want you to be uninformed, brothers, about the hardships we suffered in the province of Asia. We were under great pressure, far beyond our ability to endure, so that we despaired even of*

> *life. Indeed, in our hearts we felt the sentence of death. But this happened that we might not rely on ourselves but on God, who raises the dead. He has delivered us from such deadly peril* [literally, from such a death], *and he will deliver us. On him we have set our hope that he will continue to deliver us. . . . NIV*

Here is a man speaking out of personal experience. He said, "We were under such pressure, we despaired of life. It was far beyond our ability to endure." Do you suppose that Paul was out of the will of God in that situation? There is no indication of that whatever. He was in the full will of God; doing the purpose of God; being used of God. And yet God permitted him to come into that situation of pressure where it seemed the very life was being pressed out of him.

Have you ever felt like that? Have you ever thought, "I can't take another step. There's not one more ounce of pressure that I can endure. God, why are you permitting this?" Well, Paul and many other servants of the Lord have been through that before you and there is a reason. God's reason is stated by Paul: "This happened that we might not rely on ourselves but on God who raises the dead."

God wants to bring us to a place where we are at the end of all confidence in ourself. Where we have reached the absolute limit of our own knowledge, our experience, our strength, our ability. We have entered into an experience of death and then, out of that death, God supernaturally moves to bring us into a resurrection which is on a far higher level than we were living on before we experienced that death. God is always leading us upwards. He is leading us onwards, but if He is going to bring us into a resurrection He has to bring us through a death.

I have experienced that in my own life. I remember I cried out to God once and I said, "God, why do you only bless the things that first die and then are resurrected?" I felt God gave me this simple answer: "Because, when I'm allowed to resurrect something, I resurrect it in the form I want it to be in."

So, if you are going to go through an experience of death, remember there is a resurrection. Remember there is a new revelation of God; a deeper, fuller knowledge of God if you will just hang on and trust Him and believe Him.

ABOUT THE AUTHOR

Derek Prince (1915–2003) was born in India of British parents. Educated as a scholar of Greek and Latin at Eton College and Cambridge University, England, he held a Fellowship in Ancient and Modern Philosophy at King's College. He also studied several modern languages, including Hebrew and Aramaic, at Cambridge University and the Hebrew University in Jerusalem.

While serving with the British army in World War II, he began to study the Bible and experienced a life-changing encounter with Jesus Christ. Out of this encounter he formed two conclusions: first, that Jesus Christ is alive; second, that the Bible is a true, relevant, up-to-date book. These conclusions altered the whole course of his life, which he then devoted to studying and teaching the Bible.

Derek's main gift of explaining the Bible and its teaching in a clear and simple way has helped build a foundation of faith in millions of lives. His non-denominational, non-sectarian approach has made his teaching equally relevant and helpful to people from all racial and religious backgrounds.

He is the author of over 50 books, 600 audio and 100 video teachings, many of which have been translated and published in more than 100 languages. His daily radio broadcast is translated into Arabic, Chinese (Amoy, Cantonese,Mandarin, Shanghainese, Swatow), Croatian, German, Malagasy, Mongolian, Russian,

Samoan, Spanish and Tongan. The radio program continues to touch lives around the world.

Derek Prince Ministries continues to reach out to believers in over 140 countries with Derek's teachings, fulfilling the mandate to keep on "until Jesus returns". This is effected through the outreaches of more than 30 Derek Prince Offices around the world, including primary work in Australia, Canada, China, France, Germany, the Netherlands, New Zealand, Norway, Russia, South Africa, Switzerland, the United Kingdom and the United States. For current information about these and other worldwide locations, visit www.derekprince.com

DEREK PRINCE MINISTRIES OFFICES WORLDWIDE

ASIA/ PACIFIC
DPM–Asia/Pacific
PO Box 2029
Christchurch 8140,
New Zealand
Tel: + 64 3 366 4443
E-mail: admin@dpm.co.nz
Web: www.dpm.co.nz and www.derekprince.in

AUSTRALIA
DPM–Australia
1st Floor, 134 Pendle Way
Pendle Hill
New South Wales 2145, Australia
Tel: + 612 9688 4488
Email: enquiries@derekprince.com.au
Web: www.derekprince.com.au

CANADA
DPM–Canada
P.O. Box 8354
Halifax, Nova Scotia B3K 5M1, Canada
Tel: + 1 902 443 9577
E-mail: enquiries.dpm@eastlink.ca
Web: www.derekprince.org

FRANCE
DPM–France
B.P. 31, Route d'Oupia,
34210 Olonzac, France
Tel: + 33 468 913872
Email: info@dpmf.net
Web: www.dpmf.net

GERMANY
DPM–Germany
Schwarzauer Str. 56
D-83308 Trostberg, Germany
Tel: + 49 8621 64146
E-mail: IBL.de@t-online.de
Web: www.ibl-dpm.net

NETHERLANDS
DPM–Netherlands
P.O. Box 349
1960 AH Heemskerk, The Netherlands
Tel: + 31 251 255 044
E-mail: info@nl.derekprince.com
Web: www.dpmnederland.nl

NORWAY
PO Box 129
Lodderfjord
N-5881, Bergen, Norway
Tel: +47 928 39855
E-mail: sverre@derekprince.no
web: www.derekprince.no

SINGAPORE
Derek Prince Publications Pte. Ltd.
P.O. Box 2046
Robinson Road Post Office
Singapore 904046
Tel: + 65 6392 1812
E-mail: dpmchina@singnet.com.sg
English web: www.dpmchina.org
Chinese web: www.ygmweb.org

SOUTH AFRICA
DPM–South Africa
P.O. Box 33367
Glenstantia 0010 Pretoria
South Africa
Tel: +27 12 348 9537
E-mail: enquiries@derekprince.co.za
Web: www.derekprince.co.za

SWITZERLAND
DPM–Switzerland
Alpenblick 8
8934 Knonau
Switzerland
Tel: + 41(0) 44 768 25 06
E-mail: dpm-ch@ibl-dpm.net
Web: www.ibl-dpm.net

UNITED KINGDOM
DPM–UK
Kingsfield, Hadrian Way
Baldock SG7 6AN
UK
Tel: + 44 (0) 1462 492100
Email: enquiries@dpmuk.org
Web: www.dpmuk.org

USA
DPM–USA
PO Box 19501
Charlotte NC 28219
USA
Tel: + 1 704 357 3556
E-mail: ContactUs@derekprince.org
Web: www.derekprince.org